KU-612-789

The Wit and Wisdom of Mark Twain

The Wit and Wisdom of Mark Twain

RUNNING PRESS
PHILADELPHIA · LONDON

Library of Congress Cataloging-in-Publication Number: 90–053463

ISBN 0-89471-984-X

This book may be ordered by mail from the publisher. Please add $1.00 for postage and handling.
But try your bookstore first!

Running Press Book Publishers
125 South Twenty-second Street, Philadelphia, Pennsylvania 19103

INTRODUCTION

The career of Mark Twain is the story of the transformation of an irreverent journalist into an American institution. Samuel Langhorne Clemens was an obscure, 29-year-old newspaper writer living in California when he adopted his pen name in 1864. His writing in those early years followed the humorous journalistic style of the period. But the daily writing taught him to master the art of storytelling, and his sharp observational wit began to assert itself. In 1865, his short story "The Celebrated Jumping Frog of Calaveras County" launched him to national fame.

Through his career, Twain used humor brilliantly to comment on manners and morals. Whether twitting European pretension in *The Innocents Abroad,* exploring the collision of childhood freedom with the adult world in *The Adventures of Huckleberry Finn,* or laying bare the follies of ignorance in *A Connecticut Yankee in King Arthur's Court,* Twain always entertained his readers as he spoke to their emotions and principles.

In his later years, Twain became a sort of national conscience. His hilarious public lectures were the most popular events of the day, and as befit the living legend he was, the press sought his opinion on every subject of general interest.

Here are quips by the public Twain – from his novels, speeches, and short pieces – and from his personal notebooks and letters as well. These are the thoughts of a unique, gifted man who always told the truth, even while spinning tall tales.

TRUTH IS STRANGER than fiction, but it is because fiction is obliged to stick to possibilities; truth isn't.

*Pudd'nhead Wilson's
New Calendar*

THE COMMON EYE sees only the outside of things, and judges by that, but the seeing eye pierces through and reads the heart and the soul, finding there capacities which the outside didn't indicate or promise, and which the other kind couldn't detect.

Joan of Arc

WORDS ARE ONLY painted fire;
a look is the fire itself.

*A Connecticut Yankee
in King Arthur's Court*

D O NOT OFFER A compliment and ask a favor at the same time. A compliment that is charged for is not valuable.

Notebook

THERE IS A MORAL sense and there is an immoral sense. History shows that the moral sense enables us to see morality and how to avoid it, and that the immoral sense enables us to perceive immorality and how to enjoy it.

Pudd'nhead Wilson's New Calendar

W ORK CONSISTS OF
whatever a body is
obliged to do. . . . Play
consists of whatever a body is
not obliged to do.

The Adventures of
Tom Sawyer

THE WORK THAT IS
really a man's own work
is play and not work at all.

The New York Times
November 26, 1905

THERE IS PROBABLY
no pleasure equal
to the pleasure of climbing
a dangerous Alp; but it is
a pleasure which is confined
strictly to people who can
find pleasure in it.

A Tramp Abroad

WHAT'S THE USE you learning to do right, when it's troublesome to do right and ain't no trouble to do wrong, and the wages is just the same?

The Adventures of Huckleberry Finn

WE GET OUR
morals from books.
I didn't get mine from books,
but I know that morals do
come from books—
theoretically, at least.

"Remarks at the Opening
of the Mark Twain Library"

Y OU CAN'T PRAY
a lie.

*The Adventures of
Huckleberry Finn*

THE LIE, AS A
. . . virtue, a principle,
is eternal; the lie, as a
recreation, a solace, a refuge
in time of need, the fourth
Grace, the tenth Muse, man's
best and surest friend, is
immortal . . .

"On the Decay of
the Art of Lying"

HOMELY TRUTH is unpalatable.

The Adventures of
Tom Sawyer

I WAS GRATIFIED TO BE able to answer promptly, and I did. I said I didn't know.

Life on the Mississippi

THERE IS NOTHING IN the world like a persuasive speech to fuddle the mental apparatus.

"The Man That
Corrupted
Hadleyburg"

PROPHECIES which promise valuable things, desirable things, good things, worthy things, never come true. Prophecies of this kind are like wars fought in a good cause – they are so rare that they don't count.

Mark Twain's
Autobiography

ALWAYS DO RIGHT. This will gratify some people, and astonish the rest.

"To the Young People's Society, Greenpoint Presbyterian Church, Brooklyn"

I NEVER DID A THING IN ALL my life, virtuous or otherwise, that I didn't repent of in twenty-four hours.

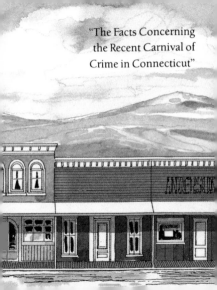

"The Facts Concerning
the Recent Carnival of
Crime in Connecticut"

I HAVEN'T A particle of confidence in a man who has no redeeming petty vices.

IT'S NOBLE TO BE GOOD, and it's nobler to teach others to be good, and less trouble.

"Remarks at the Opening of the Mark Twain Library"

WHEN I REFLECT upon the number of disagreeable people who I know have gone to a better world, I am moved to lead a different life.

Pudd'nhead Wilson's
Calendar

YOU CAN'T MAKE A
life over – society
wouldn't let you if you would.

The Gilded Age

ITS NAME IS PUBLIC
Opinion. It is held in
reverence. It settles everything. Some think it is
the voice of God.

*Europe and
Elsewhere*

HABIT IS HABIT and not to be flung out of the window by any man but coaxed down-stairs a step at a time.

Pudd'nhead Wilson's
Calendar

WE CAN'T ALL BE sound: we've got to be the way we're made.

Tom Sawyer Abroad

CLOTHES MAKE THE man. Naked people have little or no influence in society.

Notebook

HAIN'T WE GOT ALL the fools in town on our side? And hain't that a big enough majority in any town?

The Adventures of Huckleberry Finn

LET US BE THANKFUL for the fools. But for them the rest of us could not succeed.

Pudd'nhead Wilson's
New Calendar

THE COUNTRY IS THE real thing, the substantial thing, the eternal thing, it is the thing to watch over and care for and be loyal to; institutions are extraneous . . .

A Connecticut Yankee in King Arthur's Court

IT COULD PROBABLY BE shown by facts and figures that there is no distinctly native American criminal class except Congress.

Pudd'nhead Wilson's
New Calendar

ONLY WHEN
a republic's *life*
is in danger should a man
uphold his government
when it is in the wrong.
There is no other time.

"Glances at History
(suppressed)"

I T IS BY THE GOODNESS
  of God that in our country
we have those three un-
speakably precious things:
freedom of speech, freedom
of conscience, and the
prudence never to practice
either of them.

More Tramps Abroad

T O SOME PEOPLE
it is fatal to be noticed
by greatness.

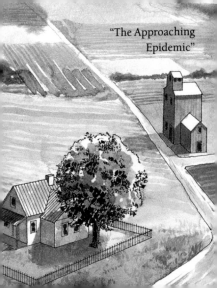

"The Approaching Epidemic"

WE DON'T CARE TO eat toadstools that think they are truffles.

Pudd'nhead Wilson's
Calendar

GOOD BREEDING consists in concealing how much we think of ourselves and how little we think of the other person.

Notebook

I T IS EASY TO FIND fault, if one has that disposition. There was once a man who, not being able to find any other fault with his coal, complained that there were too many prehistoric toads in it.

Pudd'nhead Wilson's Calendar

THERE AIN'T NO WAY
to find out why a snorer
can't hear himself snore.

Tom Sawyer Abroad

FEW OF US CAN STAND prosperity. Another man's, I mean.

Pudd'nhead Wilson's
New Calendar

SOAP AND EDUCATION are not as sudden as a massacre, but they are more deadly in the long run.

"The Facts Concerning
the Recent Resignation"

THE ELASTIC HEART
of youth cannot be
compressed into one
constrained shape long
at a time.

The Adventures
of Tom Sawyer

THERE HAS NEVER been an intelligent person of the age of sixty who would consent to live his life over again. His or anyone else's.

Letters from
the Earth

*N*OTHING REMAINS the same. When a man goes back to look at the house of his childhood, it has always *shrunk*: there is no instance of such a house being as big as the picture in memory and imagination calls for.

Letter to
William Dean Howells
[August 22, 1887]

CONSIDER WELL THE proportions of things.

It is better to be a young June-bug than an old bird of paradise.

Pudd'nhead Wilson's Calendar

THE DREAMER'S valuation of a thing lost – not another man's – is the only standard to measure it by, and his grief for it makes it large and great and fine, and is worthy of our reverence in all cases.

"My Boyhood Dreams"

EPITAPHS ARE CHEAP, and they do a poor chap a world of good after he is dead, especially if he had hard luck while he was alive. I wish they were used more.

"A Curious Dream"

THE BEST WAY TO
cheer yourself is to try
to cheer someody else up.

Notebook

WRINKLES SHOULD merely indicate where smiles have been.

Pudd'nhead Wilson's
New Calendar

AFTER ALL THESE years, I see that I was mistaken about Eve in the beginning; it is better to live outside the Garden with her than inside without her. . . . I should be sorry to have that voice fall silent and pass out of my life.

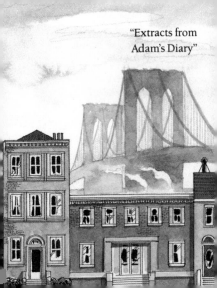
"Extracts from
Adam's Diary"

FAMILIARITY BREEDS
contempt – and
children.

Notebook

GRIEF CAN TAKE
care of itself; but to get
the full value of a joy you
must have someone to divide
it with.

Pudd'nhead Wilson's
New Calendar

TROUBLES ARE ONLY mental; it is the mind that manufactures them, and the mind can forget them, banish them, abolish them.

Which Was It?

COURAGE IS
resistance to fear,
mastery of fear – not absence
of fear.

Pudd'nhead Wilson's
Calendar

O PTIMIST:
day-dreamer

more elegantly spelled.

Notebook

HAPPINESS AIN'T A *thing in itself* – it's only a *contrast* with something that ain't pleasant.

"Captain Stormfield's
Visit to Heaven"

MAN IS THE ONLY
animal that blushes.

Or needs to.

Pudd'nhead Wilson's
New Calendar

W HAT DO YOU call love, hate, charity, revenge, humanity, magnanimity, forgiveness? Different results of the one master impulse: the necessity of securing one's self-approval.

What is Man?

No one is willing to acknowledge a fault in himself when a more agreeable motive can be found for the estrangement of his acquaintances.

The Gilded Age

I T IS CURIOUS—
curious that physical

courage should be so

common in the world, and

moral courage so rare.

Mark Twain
in Eruption

THE HOLY PASSION OF friendship is of so sweet and steady and loyal and enduring a nature that it will last through a lifetime, if not asked to lend money.

Pudd'nhead Wilson's Calendar

THE LACK OF MONEY
is the root of all evil.

Notebook

I F YOU PICK UP A starving dog and make him prosperous, he will not bite you. This is the principal difference between a dog and a man.

Pudd'nhead Wilson's
Calendar

I USED TO WORSHIP
the mighty genius of
Michaelangelo – that man
who was great in poetry,
painting, sculpture, archi-
tecture – great in everything
he undertook. But I do not
want Michaelangelo for
breakfast . . . . I like a change,
occasionally.

The Innocents Abroad

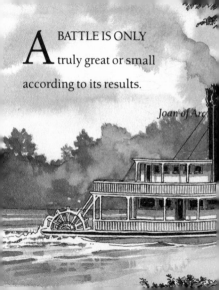

A BATTLE IS ONLY truly great or small according to its results.

Joan of Arc

ALL I CARE TO KNOW is that a man is a human being—that is enough for me; he can't be much worse.

"Concerning the Jews"

I T IS DIFFERENCE
of opinion that makes

horse races.

Pudd'nhead Wilson's
Calendar

I MUST HAVE A prodigious quantity of mind; it takes me as much as a week, sometimes, to make it up.

The Innocents Abroad

THE MAN WITH A new idea is a crank until the idea succeeds.

Pudd'nhead Wilson's
New Calendar

THERE'S ALWAYS a hole in theories somewhere, if you look close enough.

Tom Sawyer Abroad

A SOUTHERNER
talks music.

*Life on the
Mississippi*

DO NOT PUT OFF TILL tomorrow what can be put off till day-after-tomorrow just as well.

Notebook

SHUT THE DOOR. NOT that it lets in the cold but that it lets out the cozyness.

Notebook

TRAINING IS everything. The peach was once a bitter almond; cauliflower is nothing but cabbage with a college education.

Pudd'nhead Wilson's Calendar

"CLASSIC." A BOOK which people praise and don't read.

Pudd'nhead Wilson's
New Calendar

YOU CAN FIND IN A
text whatever you bring,
if you will stand between it
and the mirror of your
imagination. You may not see
your ears, but they are there.

"A Fable"

THUNDER IS GOOD,
thunder is impressive;
but it is lightning that does
the work.

Letter to an
Unidentified Person
[1908]

IT IS BEST TO READ THE weather forecast before we pray for rain.

Notebook

FOR ALL THE TALK you hear about knowledge being such a wonderful thing, instink is worth forty of it for real unerringness.

Tom Sawyer Abroad

GET YOUR FACTS first . . . then you can distort 'em as much as you please.

Quoted by
Rudyard Kipling in
From Sea to Shining Sea

THERE ARE THREE kinds of lies: lies, damned lies, and statistics.

Mark Twain's
Autobiography

TRUTH IS THE MOST valuable thing we have.

Let us economize it.

Pudd'nhead Wilson's
New Calendar

EVERY MAN IS IN HIS own person the whole human race without a detail lacking. . . . I knew I should not find in any philosophy a single thought which had not passed through my own head, nor a single thought which had not passed through the heads of millions and millions of men before I was born . . .

Mark Twain
in Eruption

WE SHOULD BE careful to get out of an experience only the wisdom that is in it – and stop there; lest we be like the cat that sits down on a hot stove-lid. She will never sit down on a hot stove-lid again – and that is well; but also she will never sit down on a cold one any more.

Pudd'nhead Wilson's New Calendar

AGAINST THE assault of laughter

nothing can stand.

The Mysterious
Stranger

This book has been bound using handcraft methods, and Smyth-sewn to ensure durability.

The dust jacket was designed
by Toby Schmidt.
The front cover was illustrated
by Charles Santore.
The back cover art was provided
by North Wind Picture Archives.
The interior was designed by
Judith Barbour Osborne.
The interior was illustrated
by Gary Undercuffler.
The text was set in Berkeley Oldstyle by
Commcor Communications Corporation,
Philadelphia, Pennsylvania.